Prayers
for
Your Day

AUBREY COLEMAN

Contents

PRAYERS FOR *the Morning*

Snooze Button

Heavenly Father,

*Help me to surrender every minute
of this day to You.*

Remind me that this day is Yours.

*Help me to lay aside the weight of yesterday
and to receive this day with eager expectation.*

As the alarm sounds, may I think first of You.

*May it serve as a blaring reminder that
You have given me another day.*

May I delight in Your new morning mercies.

*Grant me the wisdom and energy not to
waste a single moment.*

This day is Yours.

Amen

Getting Ready for the Day

The Preparer of Days,

Help me to be prepared for Your work today.

*As I glimpse into the mirror, may I
remember who I belong to.*

May I be reminded of the image I bear.

May I serve as a reflection of Jesus to those around me.

*May I be armored in your Word, and may I
be utterly dependent on prayer.*

*Help me to prepare for this day as an
ambassador of Christ.*

Help me to serve and love others well.

*Help me refrain from aiming to glorify myself;
instead, turn my heart toward Your glory.*

I thank You, Lord, for another day.

Amen

Morning Coffee

Heavenly Father,

Thank You for Your simple gifts.

*Thank You for the delight I find in
this warm cup of coffee.*

*You remind me in the quiet of the morning,
in the pause of each sip, that You renew
our strength each morning.*

*May this simple gift point me to my
greatest need in You.*

*Before I run to refuel with caffeine, may I first
run to be refueled in Your Word, Lord.*

*May I wake up with craving and longing
for Your Word.*

*With morning coffee as a kind companion,
help me to delight in You today.*

Amen

Making Your Bed

Heavenly Father,

Help me to begin my day with careful discipline.

*Help me to be a faithful steward of
what You have given me.*

*Remind me of the importance
of doing small things.*

*As I pull the sheets into their proper places, may I be
reminded of the importance of faithful habits.*

*May I begin the day with routines and habits
that encourage spiritual growth and
the development of disciplines.*

*As I look at the freshly made bed,
may I delight in good work.*

*May I be encouraged to steward my
home and life well.*

*And may I ultimately be reminded that
God has equipped me in every way to
serve Him faithfully.*

Amen

Watching the Sunrise

God of Creation,

*What a marvel it is to see the sun
peeking over the horizon.*

*You light the sky each morning and bring
us the hope of a new day.*

*You remind us of Your steadfast love that never
ceases by placing the sun into the sky.*

*Psalm 113:3 says, "From the rising of the sun to its
setting, let the name of the Lord be praised."*

*May I declare the faithful work of
Your hands every morning!*

*May the sunrise lead me to worship
Your holy name.*

Thank you for Your creative wonders.

Lord, I praise You for this day!

Amen

Before Social Media

Heavenly Father,

*You have given us creative ways to connect
with others, and I am so grateful.*

Social media can be useful when we use it well.

*But remind us of its dangers when we run to
it without restraint.*

*Give us wisdom and understanding as we
look to the lives of others.*

*Help us to flee from covetous thoughts
toward our neighbor.*

*Help us to share and write in a way that is
profitable to others and builds them up.*

*Help us not to be boastful or deceitful
in what we display.*

*In moments of quiet and boredom, lead us
away from mindlessly scrolling.*

*Help us to fill our time with things that are
fruitful and productive.*

*Help us not to run to social media first thing
but to meditate on Your Word.*

*May the foundation of our thoughts not be
filled with images of our feed but grounded
in truth, honor, purity, and love.*

Amen

PRAYERS FOR *Chores + daily routines*

Dishes

Gracious God,

*As I do this tedious task, may it provide me
a moment to pause and look to You.*

You are faithful in the big things and in the small things.

*Never once have you removed Your hand
from the lives of Your children.*

*Just as we come to the sink time and time
again to clean the dishes, so You continuously
cleanse our hearts from unrighteousness that
we may look more like Your Son.*

Though we grow tired, You never do.

You are always preparing and shaping us.

You delight in drawing near to us time and time again.

*May these moments of rinsing dishes remind us of
the opportunity you have given us to serve.*

*May we see that You are providing a way to
care for our home and serve our family.*

*Help us not to view this as a daunting task but as an
occasion to reflect Your continual care for us.*

May we, by Your grace, receive it with gratitude.

Amen

Laundry

Heavenly Father,

*Thank You for clothing. I thank You for providing
for our family in a way that gives warmth
and covering to our bodies.*

*Every piece of clothing I fold is another reminder
of Your provision for us.*

*You tell us in Your Word not to be anxious about
what we will wear but to seek first Your kingdom
and righteousness (Matthew 6:33).*

*You, time and time again, reveal Your
continuous care for us.*

*But I confess I can forget Your care and instead become
frustrated by the chore of washing, drying, folding,
and returning clothes to their places.*

*I grow weary of the countless articles of clothing
that need to go through the cycle.*

*I often approach this chore with hesitation,
assuming it will take up my time.*

*But Lord, reveal my selfish tendencies, and
enable me to serve.*

*Remind me of the gift we have been given in
baskets of clothing.*

*Help me to turn moments of grumbling into
moments of gratitude.*

*Help me to use this time to serve my family
and praise You for Your provision.*

Amen

Cleaning

The Maker of All Things New,

*You teach us about Yourself even
in our daily chores.*

*I pray this chore of cleaning brings to mind
the truth of Your Word.*

*May it serve as a metaphor for your
commitment to making us new.*

*You say in Your Word, "Therefore, if anyone is in
Christ, he is a new creation; the old has passed away,
and see, the new has come!" (2 Corinthians 5:17).*

*May I look to the sparkling countertops,
the swept floors, the tidy rooms, and the
dusted shelves and be reminded of how
beautiful it is to make things new.*

*May it encourage me to be faithful to cleaning
daily, even when it feels monotonous.*

*Lord, may my chores bring quiet moments to
consider Your work in my life.*

*May it provide a pause in my day to remember
Your faithfulness to me.*

Amen

Preparing Meals

Heavenly Father,

You give abundantly.

*As I lay out the ingredients to prepare a meal,
I thank You for providing food.*

*I thank You that we can create meals and
delight in what we eat.*

I thank You that we are not left hungry or thirsty.

*Lord, everything we have been given to nourish
our bodies has been provided by You.*

Thank You for supplying our needs.

*As I prepare this meal, Lord, I pray that it
nourishes our bodies to serve You.*

*I pray the hands that feast on this meal are
opened to delight in Your work.*

*I pray this meal that provides temporary
sustenance will point us to You as our
ultimate and eternal Sustainer.*

*I pray this meal provides energy to accomplish
Your purposes today.*

Lord, prepare my heart as I prepare this meal.

Give me a willing and serving spirit.

Help me to honor You in all things.

Amen

Running Errands

Heavenly Father,

*Thank You for a spare amount of time
to get a few things done.*

I treasure this gift of time You have given me.

I often make lists and have things that need to be done.

*Whenever I'm running errands, I confess that
I can be selfish with my time.*

*If I'm interrupted in my to-do list, I am
tempted to become angry.*

*If things do not run according to plan, I am
tempted to be unkind to others.*

*If I do not get everything done, I can become
irritable and impatient.*

*Lord, help me to pause and remember that
You have provided this time for me.*

*Help me to consider the opportunities You
may provide for me during this time.*

*Grant me the patience and understanding if
everything does not go as planned.*

*Help me to be productive and efficient so that
I can steward this time well.*

*And Lord, keep my eyes open to ways to display
Your love to those around me.*

*In moments when it seems no one is watching,
help me to represent You well.*

*I pray that I am a faithful servant even
while running errands.*

Amen

Taking Kids to School

Father,

Remind me that every moment matters.

Even in this short amount of time that I am taking the kids to school, You have provided time to make eternal investments.

Lord, may You prepare our hearts for this day.

May You provide my children with wisdom and discernment today.

May You give them attentive minds and an eagerness to learn.

May You spur them on toward kindness and love of their neighbor.

May You keep Your Word fresh in their hearts to help them combat sin and walk in obedience.

May they be reminded of Your continued presence throughout the day.

Lord, protect them from harm and evil.

Give me confidence in Your never-ending love and care for them when I am afraid.

Allow me to trust Your steady hand in their lives while I am away from them.

Help us to rejoice in this new day You have given us and to use it for Your glory.

Amen

Working Out

Father,

As I prepare my workout, I come first to You.

*You have given me muscles and strength and
the ability to move.*

I praise You for this body You have formed and made.

Help me not to take it for granted.

*Lord, help me to steward it well through
exercise and healthy habits.*

*Give me the endurance to push through a workout
even when I want to give up.*

*Give me the energy to commit time and effort
toward a work-out even when I'm tired.*

*In all things, even as I sweat and challenge
myself physically, help me to do all things
to the glory of Your name.*

*Remind me of the value found in bodily exercise,
but even more so, remind me of the
eternal value of godliness.*

*May this workout prepare me for this day,
and may the truth of Your Word prepare me for
this life and the life to come.*

Amen

Gardening

Creator God,

*What a gift that You have given us the role of
caring for Your creation.*

*You have chosen us to work the ground
and cultivate the soil.*

*As we plant seeds and wait for growth, Lord,
remind us that You alone bring life.*

*You alone bring growth to the flowers, the trees,
the fruits, and the vegetables.*

Yet, You allow us to nurture and care for their growth.

*Remind us in the tedious moments of pulling weeds,
that we are making more room for growth, just as uprooting
sin gives room for righteousness in our lives.*

*Remind us as we continually need to water plants, that we
are quenching their need for water, just as drinking from
Your Word quenches our thirst for living water.*

*Lord, help us look for all of the ways
creation speaks of Your glory.*

*May our work in the garden leave us in
awe and worship of You.*

*Though growth takes time, help us to remain
faithful to the task at hand.*

*Help us to grow in patience and hopeful expectation
of what You will accomplish over time.*

Amen

PRAYERS FOR *work*

Productivity

Heavenly Father,

Thank You for providing work for me.

I ask that You mentally prepare me to be productive today.

*I acknowledge that my mind is not always focused,
and some days are filled with distractions.*

*I am tempted to reach for my phone too often or
overthink the needs of the day.*

I am tempted to waste my time and accomplish very little.

*Help me to be a good steward of my time and to
be diligent with the tasks at hand.*

Help me to get done what needs to be completed today.

*Help my mind to remain sharp and my energy
to be sustained.*

*Remind me of Your strength in moments
when I feel weak and weary.*

Remind me of Your ever-present help in times of need.

*Grant me the willingness to work wholeheartedly
unto You, Lord, and to accomplish all that You
desire for me to accomplish today.*

Amen

Engaging with Co-workers

Father,

Thank You for allowing me to work alongside others.

Thank You for the gift of working in community.

*Lord, though I know my coworkers are a gift, I confess
I do not always treat them as such.*

*I confess that I can grow impatient when
others are not efficient.*

I can be critical of others who think differently than I do.

I can be unkind when things do not go my way.

*Remind me that You have made each of my coworkers
to contribute uniquely and purposefully.*

*Remind me that I am limited in my own
perspective and abilities.*

*Help me to learn from their different perspectives
and work ethics.*

Help me to find joy in our collaborative efforts.

Grant me humility and patience toward my coworkers.

Help me to be kind and encouraging to others.

*Help me to engage with my coworkers in a way
that is honoring and glorifying to You.*

Amen

Listening to Your Boss

Father,

I lift up my boss in prayer today.

Thank You for gifting him with the ability to lead.

I pray You continue to give him the wisdom and discernment to lead his employees well.

I pray You give him the gifting and ability to fulfill his role completely.

Lord, in Your sovereignty, You ordained for me to work under his leadership.

Though I trust in Your provision, I confess at times, I may find it difficult to listen to my boss's direction. I confess I may not always agree with his decisions. I confess I am tempted to be critical of his judgment and leadership.

But Lord, help me to remain respectful and honorable as an employee.

Help me to trust in the authority You have placed over me.

Help me to be a support and help to my boss.

Help me to be a listener and a learner.

Remind me of Your ultimate, sovereign care in all things.

Help me to trust my boss while I ultimately trust in You.

Amen

Weight of Demands

Father,

What a gift it is to call on You in times of need.

Thank You for always listening to our prayers.

*Thank You for always providing help
and comfort for us.*

*Lord, I confess I am overwhelmed by the
weight of demands today.*

*I feel unprepared and unable to
accomplish everything.*

I find myself becoming anxious and stressed.

I feel myself wearing thin at my incapabilities.

*Lord, You say in Your Word that when we
are weak, You are strong.*

Remind me of the strength I will find in You.

*Lord, You say in Your Word to cast all our
burdens on You because You care for us.*

Remind me to give my burdens to You.

*Help me to prioritize what needs to be done
today and trust in You with the rest.*

I pray You will provide relief for me today.

Amen

PRAYERS FOR *Bible Study*

Before Spending Time in Scripture

Heavenly Father,

Thank You for the gift of Your Word.

*Lord, bring me great delight and joy
in Your Word today.*

*Help me to search it with fervor and zeal
to know You more.*

Open my eyes to see marvelous things in Your Word!

*Teach me through the power of the Holy Spirit
the truths You would have me learn.*

*Plant Your words deep in my heart so that
I might not sin against You.*

*Help me not only to be a hearer but a
doer of Your Word.*

*Grant me wisdom and understanding
through truths of Your law.*

*Help me to treasure the riches I find and
apply them to my days.*

*Sanctify me in Your truth, and leave me
hungering for Your Word again.*

Amen

When You Don't Understand a Passage

Father,

*I come to You confused by the passage I read,
and I am unable to understand the
meaning of the text.*

*I pray my misunderstandings would draw me
closer to seek wisdom and truth from You.*

*Help me not to grow frustrated or weary
in my limitations, but may my weakness
propel me into Your strength.*

*I ask that You help me, through the work
of the Spirit, to behold wondrous
things in Your Word.*

*I ask that You open my eyes to understand
the truths revealed among these pages.*

*Lord, please give me knowledge and insight
into what You would have me learn
from this passage today.*

You say Your Word will never return void.

*Lord, I pray You bear fruit in my life from
what I have read today even
when I don't understand.*

Amen

When Studying with Others

Heavenly Father,

*It is a joy and a privilege to study Your Word
with others, and I thank You for the opportunity.*

It is a gift to read the Bible in community with others.

*Lord, prepare my heart to learn and grow from
the thoughts and views of others.*

*Guard me against pride or a desire to boast
in my own understanding.*

Open my eyes to see new things in Your Word today.

Remind me of my own limitations.

*Help me to grow in appreciation of the different
perceptions You have given Your people. Help me to be
encouraged and strengthened by the different lives and
experiences You have given to each of us.*

*Help me to gain a better understanding of
You and Your purposes.*

Lord, I pray this time would be fruitful for each of us.

*I pray you would refuel and refresh our souls
with Your knowledge and wisdom.*

*I pray we would leave our time together better
prepared to glorify and honor You in all we do.*

Amen

When Preparing to Lead the Time

Father,

I come before You preparing to lead a Bible study.

*I pray You would help me to prepare
for our time diligently.*

*Help me to cling to Your Word as I aim to rightly
handle my teaching material.*

*I ask that You prepare my heart to teach humbly
and be utterly dependent on You.*

*I ask that You remove any pride
or arrogance in my heart.*

*I ask that You remove any fear or
nervousness I may feel.*

*Help me not to speak out of my own wisdom but out
of the truth and knowledge of Your Word.*

*I acknowledge my limitations and pray You
would strengthen me in Your Spirit.*

Embolden me to speak Your Word in confidence.

*Help me to cling to You for knowledge
and understanding.*

Help me to teach in a way that is profitable and faithful.

*I pray You prepare the hearts and minds of those
I'm studying the Bible with today.*

*I ask that You teach us new things from Your
Word and grow us in godliness.*

*May we be encouraged by our time together and leave
knowing You more deeply than when we came.*

Amen

After Spending Time in Scripture

Heavenly Father,

Thank You for the time to spend in Your Word.

"How sweet your word is to my taste, sweeter than honey on my mouth!" (Psalm 119:103).

Remind me of its sweetness every waking moment, and leave me longing to return to savor it.

Lord, I pray You would plant Your Word down deep in my heart and cause it to bear fruit in my life.

Help me to encourage others in the truths I have learned.

Help me to remember Your Word when I am tempted to sin against You.

Remind me that You have the words of eternal life.

May they be engraved in my heart and mind.

May I cling to them with every part of me.

Amen

PRAYERS FOR *the evening*

Sharing a Meal

Heavenly Father,

We thank you for this meal shared together.

*It is by Your grace that we can gather and enjoy
time with one another.*

*We thank you for the food You have provided for us and
the hands that have graciously prepared it for us.*

*We pray you would bless our conversations and
provide encouraging fellowship.*

*Just as you broke bread and ate with Your disciples,
remind us of the privilege and joy it is to share
a meal with others.*

May we honor You in everything we say and do.

May this time be rich and refueling for each of us.

We love You and praise You for this time together.

Amen

Before Screens

Father,

Thank You for entertainment and moments to enjoy it.

*Thank You for the gift that our screens can
be when we use them well.*

*Lord, we pray as we turn on our television,
computers, or tablets, that we would intentionally
tune our hearts to Your glory.*

Help us to be thoughtful about what we fill our minds with.

Keep us from engaging in any sinful thoughts or attitudes.

*Protect us from any temptation to indulge in
our fleshly desires.*

*Help us to watch, listen, and learn in a way
that seeks to honor and glorify You.*

Lord, help us restrain from excessive screen time.

*Give us wisdom and discernment for when it is
time to turn off our screens.*

Amen

Watching the Sunset

God of Creation,

You display Your faithfulness to us in beautiful ways.

*As the bright and shining sun falls to touch the
horizon, I am reminded of another day You have
brought to completion – another day numbered
in Your book, another day filled with Your purposes
and plans prepared before the foundation of the earth.*

*Lord, I praise You for all that You have
accomplished on this day.*

*I praise You for the simple joys You have
given us to enjoy.*

*I thank You for every opportunity You have
given us to learn and grow.*

*May the setting of the sun always remind me of
Your faithfulness to carry us through each day.*

Help me to know and love You even more tomorrow.

Amen

Evening Walk

Heavenly Father,

I praise You for the simple joy of an evening walk.

*I praise You for time to step away from the workday
and obligations at home.*

*Allow this time to step away from the distractions
of the world and spend time with You.*

*Lord, remind me in these moments that You walk
with me every step of the way.*

Draw me closer to You in times of quiet and solitude.

Rid my thoughts of any anxiety, doubts, or fear.

*Help me to think on whatever is true, honorable,
just, pure, lovely, and commendable.*

Help me to rest in Your steadfast love and faithfulness to me.

Bring me peace and calm on this evening walk.

May I end this day in heartfelt gratitude to You.

Amen

Before Bed

Lord of Days,

As the day comes to a close, Lord, I thank You for rest.

When the days are long and tiresome,
You provide us with the gift of sleep.

You allow our minds to slow and our bodies to calm.

Lord, help me to cast all my cares on You.

Help me to relinquish the burdens and
the hardships of the day.

Help me to entrust my thoughts and worries to You.

Remind me of my limitations as I rest my head
and search for sleep.

Though I need sleep, Lord, You never sleep or slumber.

You are not limited or confined by weakness.

Your care for us is unending, and You keep watch
over us through the night.

Prepare my heart to receive Your new
mercies in the morning, and equip me to
serve You faithfully tomorrow.

Amen

PRAYERS FOR *the week*

Start of a New Week

Heavenly Father,

I pray You would help me prepare for this week well.

Lord, remind me that every day ordained for me has been written in Your book before it comes to be.

You know what this week holds and prepared it before the foundations of the earth.

Help me to trust and depend on You for my days.

Help me to fill my time with devotion and prayer.

Help me to give my time freely and humbly to serve others.

Grant me opportunities to share the gospel with those I interact with this week.

Help me to open up my home freely and show hospitality generously.

Give me strength and grace to love and care for my family well.

Allow me productivity and efficiency in what needs to be accomplished this week.

Teach me to number my days so that I will seek wisdom and discernment with how best to use my time.

And in whatever I do, Lord, I hope to do it all for the glory of Your name.

Amen

End of a Week

Father,

Another week You have brought to completion.

We thank You for the days You have given to us.

Each one was intentional and purposeful
in Your plan for our lives.

Whether hardship or joy, Lord, You are using
every moment to teach us.

We praise You for never wasting a moment to
sanctify us into the likeness of Your Son.

Lord, You are good and faithful.

The ending of this week is another example
of Your faithfulness to us.

You have carried us through the long days
and busy schedules.

And we can rest assured You will continue to do so.

Help us not to rush into planning the days ahead.

Instead, help us to take time to rest and refuel for
another week to come and to reflect on Your
continued presence and provision in our lives.

Amen

Sunday Rest

Father of Rest,

*Just as You created the heavens and the earth and
every living thing to then take a moment to rest,*

so You have given us a day of rest.

*You have given us a day to gather with Your people and
to worship Your name with singing, praying, reading
Your Word, and fellowshipping with one another.*

Help us to soak up the teaching of Your Word.

Help us to rejoice and praise You in song.

*Help us to cast our cares on You and lift up
Your name in prayer.*

*Help us to be encouraged and spurred
on by Your people.*

*May this day provide us with a fresh perspective
and a heart in tune with the glory of God.*

*May this day clear our minds from the previous weeks
and bring rest to our weary and restless bodies.*

*May it equip and prepare us to face the coming days as
laborers of Christ, living in the world but not of the world,
seeking to know, love, and enjoy God more and more.*

*Lord, help us not to neglect this day but to treasure
it as the day You have given us to rest.*

Amen

For My Spouse

Heavenly Father,

I praise You for my spouse.

*I praise You for choosing us to seek your
glory in this life together.*

*I thank You for the gift of friendship and
companionship we find in one another.*

*You have given us immeasurable joy and
delight in one another.*

*I pray You continue to sustain that joy
for the rest of our days.*

Lord, use our marriage to honor You.

*And continue to grow us and sanctify us
into the likeness of Christ.*

*I pray specifically for my spouse that he
would desire to know You more.*

Lord, give him a hunger for Your Word.

Give him a thirst for Your righteousness.

Help him to seek You for discernment in every decision.

*Surround him with wise counsel to guide us
through hard seasons.*

*Lord, help him to hone his giftings to the
glory of Your name.*

*Help him to see the unique and wonderful
ways you have created him.*

Tune his heart to seek after You in everything he does.

Hold our marriage fast for the rest of our days.

Amen

As a Spouse

Heavenly Father

*I praise You for marriage and the beautiful picture
it presents of Christ and the church.*

*I thank you for the opportunity to love and serve
my spouse in ways that reflect that.*

*Lord, help me to continue learning more and
more about my spouse each day.*

*Help me to be quick to listen, slow to speak,
and slow to become angry.*

Use every opportunity to sanctify me into Your likeness.

Help me to sharpen my spouse in truth.

Help me to also be sharpened by him in truth.

*Create in me a generous and humble heart
that seeks his interest above my own.*

Grant me a willingness to apologize and seek forgiveness.

*Help me to be an encouragement to my spouse,
always looking for ways to spur him on and build
him up in the faith.*

Lord, give me a hunger and thirst for Your Word.

Give me a thirst for Your righteousness.

Help me to seek You for discernment in every decision.

*Surround me with wise counsel to guide me
through hard seasons.*

Help me to use my strengths to support our marriage.

Tune my heart to seek after you in everything I do.

Hold our marriage fast for the rest of our days.

Amen

iving to the Needy

"Beware of practicing your righteousness before other people in order to be seen by them, for then you will have reward from your Father who is in heaven.

"Thus, when you give to the needy, sound no trumpet e you, as the hypocrites do in the synagogues and in the s, that they may be praised by others. Truly, I say to you, ave received their reward. ³ But when you give to the do not let your left hand know what your right hand is so that your giving may be in secret. And your Father in secret will reward you.

rayer

hen you pray, you must not be like the hypocrites. e to stand and pray in the synagogues and at the s, that they may be seen by others. Truly, I say to e received their reward. ⁶ But when you pray, go n and shut the door and pray to your Father who d your Father who sees in secret will reward you. you pray, do not heap up empty phrases as for they think that they will be heard for their not be like them, for your Father knows what ou ask him. ⁹ Pray then like this:

n heaven,
our name.
come,
ne,
t is in heaven.
our daily bread,

In Moments of Frustration

Father,

I need Your help in this moment of frustration.

Keep me from responding in any sinful thought, word, or action.

Help me to assess my fault in this scenario.

Give me clear eyes to see Your truth amid my emotion.

Help me to recall Your Word to my mind so that my frustration does not lead me to respond in an ungodly way.

Give us patience and grace as my spouse and I work through conflict.

Grant us compassion and care in the words that we speak to one another.

Help us to honestly evaluate our hearts so that we might not sin against You or one another.

Lord, unite us in our pursuits to solve problems and work through hardship.

Help us to come together, encouraging one another and building one another, instead of distancing ourselves and tearing one another apart.

Allow this moment to help us depend more on You, Lord.

Allow this moment to teach us and sanctify us into the likeness of You.

We thank You for Your help, Lord.

Amen

In Moments of Joy

Heavenly Father,

We know that every moment of joy comes from You.

And we praise You for the moments of joy
You bring us in marriage.

We praise You for all of the ways You cultivate delight,
laughter, and celebration in our relationship.

We know that marriage can be hard at times,
so help us not to take for granted any
joyous occasion you give us!

Help us to celebrate and dance and sing and laugh.

Bring us greater delight in You and greater
delight in one another.

You tell us in Your Word that the joy
of the Lord is our strength.

Use these moments to renew our strength in You.

Lord, we pray in our marriage that You would outweigh
the moments of frustration with moments of joy
and that You would continually remind us
of the many gifts You have given us.

Most importantly, we pray You would always remind
us of the gift and the joy we have found in Jesus.

Amen

On Anniversaries

Sustainer of Days,

Thank You, Lord, for another year of marriage.

Thank You for the gift and treasure of spending life together.

Help us not to take for granted your continued faithfulness in sustaining our marriage year to year.

We praise You for the many celebrations and joys we have experienced this year!

We thank You for the moments of laughter and the memories we hold dear.

And we also praise You for the trials and hard circumstances You have brought us through.

Even when things have been difficult or disappointing, Lord, You have used those moments to shape us and sanctify us.

Remind us that the foundation of our marriage is You.

Our greatest need and help in our marriage is You.

Help us to love and pursue one another in the way that You have loved and pursued us.

Help us to honor and cherish one another for every day you allow us to spend together.

We pray our marriage would serve as a reflection of the gospel to all who witness our lives.

And Lord, we pray and ask that You would give us many more years together.

Amen

PRAYERS FOR *my children*

To Know and Enjoy God Forever

Father,

I commit my child to You. Thank You that because of Christ I can freely come to the throne of grace and petition on behalf of my child.

Lord, I confess that I desperately long for my child's salvation.

I pray that he would know You as his savior.

I pray that he would submit to Your lordship, now and forevermore.

Please open the eyes of his heart, and allow him to see sin and experience brokenness over it. And by Your grace, may he respond in repentance.

May he believe in the gospel and trust in the finished work of Christ.

Father, put Your Spirit in him, and empower him to walk according to the Spirit.

May he know that his chief aim is to know and enjoy You forever and that in doing so, he will lead a full and satisfying life that glorifies You.

Father, I trust in Your goodness and sovereignty, even regarding my child's salvation.

May You receive all of the praise and glory!

Amen

When They Disobey

Father,

*Forgive me when I allow my anger and frustration
to release when my child is disobedient.*

*Forgive me when I repay disobedience with
harsh words and sin on my part.*

*In moments of disobedience, Father, remind
me of my disobedient heart.*

*Lord, cause that remembrance to humble me before
my child, to love him as You love me, and to shepherd
him to repentance and reconciliation.*

*In doing so, may You allow me to model
repentance of a disobedient heart.*

Help me to give grace to my child as he is learning.

*Ultimately, may I point him to You as the One
in whom he can trust and depend on to come to
when he is disobedient, knowing that Your arms
are open, willing, and ready to forgive.*

Amen

In Moments of Frustration

Father,

Give me patience in this frustrating moment.

Remind me that you are infinitely patient with me through every mistake, every act of disobedience, and every shortcoming.

I confess that I am inclined to react to my child with anger or despair, so let Your Spirit enable me to respond with self-control, gentleness, and love.

Give me the wisdom to know how to discipline and correct.

Help me now to extend grace to my child as you have freely extended it to me.

Soften my child's heart so that she might see her sin and her need for You, and in turn, embrace Your forgiveness and grace.

Amen

In Moments of Joy

Good Father,

*I thank You that in Your presence
there is fullness of joy.*

*I pray that my child would know You and
experience the beautiful reality of this truth.*

*May he know You as his joyful Father who
desires to grow him in Christlikeness and produce
the fruit of joy in his life.*

*May his life be filled with many moments of joy,
and may each moment remind him of Your
goodness and faithfulness.*

*Lord, may worship always be his first response
in moments of delight!*

*When he encounters beauty in this world,
may he praise You.*

*No matter what his life's circumstances are,
may he praise You.*

*May all of his life be an act of worship to You,
the giver of every good and perfect gift.*

*May he see intimacy with Jesus, the source
of everlasting joy, rather than trying to find
happiness in temporary things.*

Amen

In Moments of Growth

Heavenly Father,

*For every seed I may plant, You, Lord, are the
one who makes it grow.*

I praise You for the growth I see in my child today.

*It is Your grace that empowers her obedience,
her understanding, and her maturity.*

*Keep my heart from feeling pride for the successes of my
child, and help me humbly turn to You in gratitude for every
win and every milestone, for they are all gifts from You.*

*Teach my child in all situations to depend on You,
and continue to produce transformation and growth
in her heart and life.*

Amen

When a Milestone Comes

Gracious God,

I praise You for this milestone in my child's life.

*When I delight in seeing her accomplish
something new, I get a glimpse of what it must
be for You to look on Your children
with great delight.*

Father, help me to celebrate this well.

*May this not be a moment that causes sadness or
a desire to control things that are beyond my
capabilities, but instead, may this be another day
and another moment that I am consciously
submitting my child over to You.*

*Help me to trust in Your sovereign care
and control in her life.*

*At this milestone, may I rejoice in the grace that
You have given her to take the next step ahead
and trust You for the steps You have already
traced out for her life.*

Amen

PRAYERS FOR *this season*

Motherhood

Father,

Thank You for the gift of motherhood.

Thank You for entrusting a child to my care.

*Father, I tremble at the enormous responsibility
of discipling my child to the praise of Your glory.
I need Your help!*

I need Your sustaining grace, moment by moment.

*Lord, motherhood is sanctifying. I am confronted
with my sin every single day — oh, how my natural
inclination is to choose comfort, ease, and quick fixes.*

*May my love of self be killed and replaced
by a greater affection for You.*

*May I bend lower to serve my child out of
worship to You. Help me to be the best ambassador
of Christ to this child — may my voice be gentle
and loving, my words be saturated in truth, my arms
ready to embrace, just as You have drawn me to You.*

*May I be quick to repent, quick to give thanks,
and quick to preach the gospel in word and deed.*

*Though this is a busy life season, may I not forsake
You, my First Love. May I feast on Your Word daily,
knowing that it is transforming me from one degree
of glory to another. May I put Your glory on display
in my marriage, my parenting, and my home.*

Amen

Changing Diapers

Heavenly Father,

You see me now as I change yet another diaper.

The repetition of this becomes mundane.

But as I'm cleaning my child, I realize there is a lot of mess in my own life.

Help me to see the gospel in this essential part of raising the child that You have given me to shepherd.

Would You help me to see every diaper as a reminder of You sending Your Spirit into my heart to clean it up and make it more holy?

As I clothe my child with a new diaper, remind me of the new clothing that You have given me in Christ.

You have taken all the old, messy clothes off and replaced them with new clothes to emit the fruit of the Spirit.

Amen

Singleness

Heavenly Father,

I lift up this season in prayer to You.

*At times I am confident in where You have me
in this season of singleness and trusting You.*

*But I confess there are times I doubt Your goodness
to me, and I struggle to remain content in this season.*

*Help me to believe this season is in line with
Your sovereign plan and will.*

*Remind me that nothing happens outside of
Your provision and knowledge.*

*Lord, remind me that Your intentions are only
good all the time, and everything You do is for the glory
of Your name and the good of those who love You.*

*Help me to entrust my desires to You, knowing
that You will care for them.*

Help me trust wholeheartedly in what You hold for my future.

Lord, whatever that may be, bring me contentment and peace.

Help me to continue faithfully serving You through every season.

Lord, help me to remain steadfast in the truth of Your Word.

Keep me longing for Your kingdom, and grant me patience and endurance as I wait.

Above all else, Lord, help me to love You more than anything else.

Amen

Job That I Love

Father,

*I praise You today for the job
You have given me.*

*I know that I am not promised my
job will always be one that I enjoy.*

*But Lord, I thank You now for the
opportunity to have a job that I love.*

*Help me not to take this opportunity
for granted.*

*Help me to take note of the joy and
delight You give me each day!*

*Help me steward my days well and to
work wholeheartedly unto You.*

*I ask that You allow my joy in this job to
pour out in my relationships with others.*

*But I also pray I would not idolize it
or be tempted to elevate my job over
home and family.*

*Lord, I ask that I grow and develop in
this job and that it would provide for me
in the financial ways I need it to.*

Thank You, Lord, for this undeserved gift.

Help me to use it for the glory of Your name.

Amen

Job That is Hard

Father,

I need Your help today.

Help me to appreciate the job I have been given even if it's difficult.

I know that many do not have jobs or are unable to work, and therefore, I thank You sheerly that I am able to have a job.

Help me to see the ways You provide for me through it.

Help me to search for small joys throughout the day and work with a heart of gratitude.

Lord, grant me the ability to work diligently, even when it's challenging.

Give me the wisdom and endurance to steward my time well.

Use every opportunity of difficulty to shape me into the likeness of Christ.

I ask that You would keep the burden of my job from negatively affecting my relationships with others.

Keep it from overflowing into other areas of my life.

Lord, I ask that you would stretch me and shape me through this job and that it would provide for me in the ways I need it to.

Help me to enjoy this job more, and help me use it to the glory of Your name.

Amen

Mundane

Father,

Some days are long and tedious.

I find myself struggling to persevere when every task feels the same and every day looks the same.

I confess I can grow weary in the day to day.

I confess I can grow discontent in my circumstances.

I find myself looking for change or variation in my day.

Lord, help me to desire obedience for a lifetime.

Help me to see the need for daily surrender.

Even when the work looks the same each day, help me to search for glorious moments in the mundane.

Help me to find joy in the small things.

Help me to be reminded that every day I have breath in my lungs is another day intended to serve You.

Remind me that faithfulness in the small things is preparing for me a great reward in heaven.

Help me to see each task as an investment in Your kingdom purposes.

And use each mundane moment for Your glory alone.

Give me strength and energy to persevere on the hard days.

And when I feel weary and tired, lead me to the Rock that is higher than I.

Amen

Grief and Loss

Heavenly Father,

*You draw near to comfort the broken-hearted,
and I ask that You draw near to me.*

I'm burdened with grief and heavy laden with sadness.

I come to You because I cannot carry it on my own.

I need Your help and comfort in this time of need.

I need reminders of the truth of Your Word.

*Remind me, Lord, that because of Jesus,
death has no sting.*

*Remind me that He has defeated death in full victory,
and one day it will be no more.*

*Remind me that one day there will be
no more tears and no more pain.*

*Lord, my tears are many, and my heart is heavy.
I am overwhelmed with sorrow.*

I need Your strength and grace to continue through the days.

I ask You to help me as I process this grief.

Bring healing over time, Lord.

*Help me to remember Your promises when
I am tempted to doubt.*

*May Your unfailing love surround me
today and every day.*

Use these circumstances to draw me closer to You.

Lord, even if painful, use this grief to Your glory.

Amen

Broken Relationships

Father,

I come before You lamenting a broken relationship.

At times this relationship may discourage me, cause me anger, bring me grief, or leave me feeling hopeless.

But I am reminded through the saving work of the gospel that You can redeem anyone, Lord.

You can redeem any relationship in Your timing.

I know that the only place we find reconciliation is in You.

Help us to desire to resolve our issues and to find common ground among ourselves.

Grant us compassion and humility toward one another.

Grant us wisdom and discernment as we navigate our conversations with one another.

Bring us to our knees in prayer for Your help and comfort.

Lord, change hearts in this relationship to seek peace and pursue it.

Ultimately, Lord, may this broken relationship shift our gaze heavenward to a day when all things will be restored and made new.

May we find hope in that truth as we wait.

Amen

PRAYERS FOR *when I feel...*

Argumentative

Father,

I confess that I am feeling argumentative.

I am tempted to be prideful and unkind.

I am tempted to use my words in a harmful way.

*I am tempted to desire to be right instead
of engaging fruitfully.*

*Your Word says that the Lord's servant must not be
quarrelsome but kind to everyone (2 Timothy 2:24).*

Remind me of this truth as my feelings rush over me.

*Help me to desire to reflect You and Your truth
over reflecting myself and my opinions.*

Help me to be honest and humble.

Help me to speak with patience and kindness.

*Help me to listen first and to consider the
interest of others above my own.*

*Lord, I pray You would restrain my lips from any
unwholesome talk, and grant me the wisdom and
clarity to speak peaceably in this conversation.*

Amen

Frustrated

Father,

*As I am filled with frustration, I come before
You in need of Your help.*

*I know that in the heat of my emotions,
I will be tempted to sin.*

Lord, please keep me from any ungodly response.

Help me to tame my emotions and assess my own heart.

*Expose the sinful inclinations of my heart,
and lead me to repentance.*

*Lord, remind me of the grace You have offered
me through Your Son.*

*Help me to extend that grace to others in
frustrating circumstances.*

*Help me to be a reflection of You even when situations
are difficult and hard to manage.*

*Grant me the patience to be quick to listen
and slow to speak.*

*Grant me the gentleness and kindness not to
hurt others in the midst of my frustration.*

*Lord, help me to lay my frustrations at Your feet,
trusting that You see and know beyond my
limited perspective and that You will align all
things with Your good and perfect will.*

Amen

Anxious

Heavenly Father,

Anxious thoughts consume my heart right now.

*I come before You filled with thoughts that
bring me worry, fear, and doubt.*

*My mind is prone to wander in every different direction,
and Lord, I need Your help to bring Your truth to mind.*

*You say in Your Word that You will keep the mind that
is dependent on You in perfect peace (Isaiah 26:3).*

*Help me to keep my eyes fixed on You instead of
on fears and uncertainties.*

*Help me to keep from straining my gaze toward the
"what ifs" but instead keep my thoughts steadfast in
what I know to be true about You.*

*Lord, You tell us to cast our burdens on You because
You care for us.*

*Instead of being consumed by anxious thoughts,
help me to cast them into Your hands.*

Help me to relinquish my grip on what I cannot control.

*Help me to acknowledge my weakness and lean
into Your strength.*

Comfort me with the truth of Your goodness and sovereignty.

Surround me with the unfailing truth of Your Word.

*Set me free from anxious thoughts, and help me to think
only of what is right, good, and godly.*

Amen

Overwhelmed

Father,

I feel heavy and burdened by the present circumstances.

My mind and heart are overwhelmed.

I am not sure what to think or feel or say.

Lord, help me to search for answers and understanding in You.

Help me to come to Your Word and cling to it for guidance and wisdom.

Lead me to the Rock that is higher than I (Psalm 61:2).

Give me solid ground to stand on when everything around me feels unsteady.

Remind me that nothing is too overwhelming to You, and You can bear the weight of my burdens.

Help me to cast them on You.

Lord, bring me clarity in my circumstances.

And help me to find a way forward to walk in godliness.

Amen

Disappointed

Heavenly Father,

*I know this world will be filled with
disappointments because we plan our ways
often without knowing what's best for us, and
we live in a fallen world that awaits redemption.*

*Yet even as I know this to be true, each time I face
disappointment, I am hurt and discouraged by it.*

*Lord, I pray You would remind me of Your
faithfulness to me.*

Even as I plan my ways, Lord, You establish my steps.

*And You do so in accordance with what is
good for me and glorying to You.*

Lord, remind me of Your sovereignty.

*Though disappointments may feel as if plans
and purposes are shattered, Lord, nothing happens
outside of Your rule and reign.*

*Help me cling to Your promises when I am tempted
to doubt You amid disappointing circumstances.*

*Help me to see use these moments as another
opportunity to depend on and trust in You.*

*Use this opportunity, even if painful,
to prepare me for heaven.*

Amen

Like Holding a Grudge

Father,

I am tempted at this moment to remember wrongs.

*I am tempted to hold a grudge as a means
of punishing someone.*

*But You tell us in Your Word that love does not keep
a record of wrongs and that we are to deal mercifully
with others as You have dealt mercifully with us.*

*Help me to remember the many ways You could
have held a grudge against us.*

We disobeyed You and turned away from You in sin.

*Yet, instead of making us pay for what we
had done, You sent Your one and only Son to
pay the penalty for our sins.*

*In Your love and mercy, You set us free from the debt
we owed in order to restore a relationship with You.*

*How much more then should we show mercy
and grace when we have been wronged?*

*Lord, help me to love as You love. Help me to
forgive as You forgive.*

*Rid me of any pride or unwillingness to
pursue peace and reconciliation.*

*Fill me with the Holy Spirit, and guide me
in wisdom and truth.*

*Grant me the willingness to forgive as I have been
forgiven. And help me to reflect Christ in every way.*

Amen

Defensive

Heavenly Father,

I come before You feeling defensive.

*I confess that I've put up walls to guard
myself against others.*

*I feel an unwillingness to listen and an
unwillingness to receive feedback.*

I confess I am tempted to self-preserve.

*I confess I am tempted to respond unkindly
to protect my own image.*

*Lord, please help me to see the heart issue
behind my defenses.*

Help me to be gracious and humble in my listening.

*Help me to let down my guard, trusting in
Your care and provision.*

Help me to desire to reflect Your image instead of my own.

*Remind me that I bring nothing to the table
of my salvation but my sin.*

My defenses in and of myself will never hold strong enough.

Remind me that my greatest defense is salvation in You.

You are a shield of righteousness for me.

You protect me from the flaming arrows of the evil one.

Help me to trust in your protection and care for me.

*Remind me that You will guard and watch
my life better than I can.*

Remind me of my dire need for You, Lord.

Amen

Insecure

Father,

I come before You filled with insecurity.

*I confess that my insecurity can lead me to
compare myself to others.*

It can lead me to put others down to build myself up.

I confess my insecurity can lead me to doubt Your goodness.

It can lead me to question the way You have created me.

*I confess my insecurities can leave me discontent and
discourage me from encouraging and supporting others.*

Lord, please rid me of any ungodly thought or response.

Help me to lay my insecurities at Your feet.

*Remind me of the security I know to have
through Your Son, Jesus.*

*Remind me of my position as an heir and
ambassador of Christ.*

*Remind me of the privilege and honor it is to call
out to You as Father, as Your child.*

*You say in Your Word that I am fearfully and
wonderfully made (Psalm 139:14).*

*Remind me that every facet of my being was
intentionally made for a purpose.*

*My differences, personality, body, facial features,
upbringing, culture, and everything about me was
specifically woven into Your divine will for my life.*

Help me to trust in You when I am tempted to become insecure.

*Help me to lean into my identity and
approval found in Christ.*

Bring to mind the unchanging truth of Your Word.

May I lean on it when the world wants to tell me otherwise.

Amen

PRAYERS FOR *for a...*

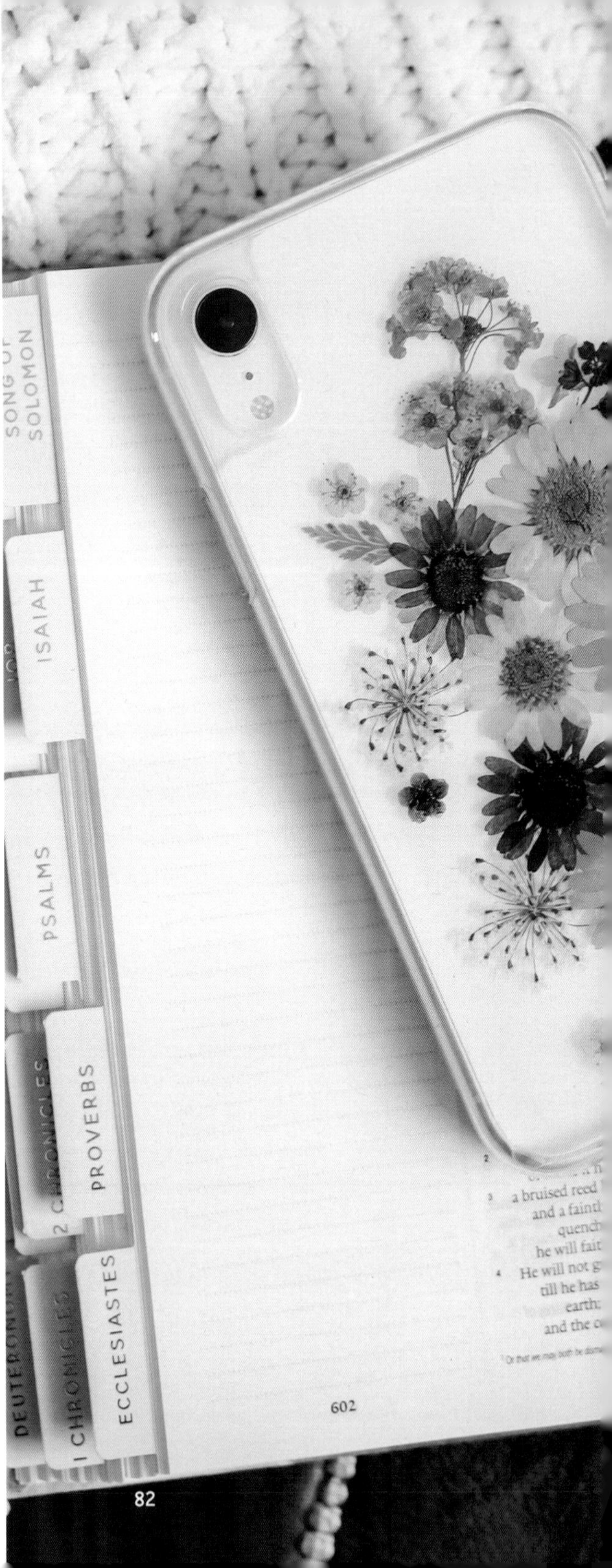

A New Pet

Heavenly Father,

What a fun and delightful gift You have given us in a new pet!

Thank You for the companionship and joy this will bring to our lives.

We know this pet will serve a special role in our home, and we praise You for bringing it into our lives.

Lord, we pray we would care for this pet well and lovingly provide for it.

Help us to grow in patience and responsibility as we spend our days caring for it.

Help us to delight in the special bond created between a pet and owner.

Help us to treasure the life of our pet to the glory of Your name!

Lord, may our life with this pet lead us to marvel at Your creation more and ultimately lead us to worship You.

Amen

A New Baby

Giver of Life,

Thank You for the beautiful gift You have given me by entrusting me with this child.

As I look at her beautiful face and delicate frame, I have a greater understanding of the magnificence of her creator whose image she bears.

May she grow to be enamored by Your goodness and love You wholeheartedly.

Empower me to be an ambassador of that love to her for as long as I live.

I know that the coming hours, days, weeks, and years will hold challenges too great for me to face on my own, and so I ask You to fill me with Your strength, Your patience, and Your wisdom.

Ease my anxieties over her tiny life because I know that You are the one who holds her together.

May every difficulty be an opportunity to depend more on You.

You are the one who gives growth, so let her mature in stature and healthy development.

But even more, draw her ever and always to Yourself so that she will grow up in You.

Amen

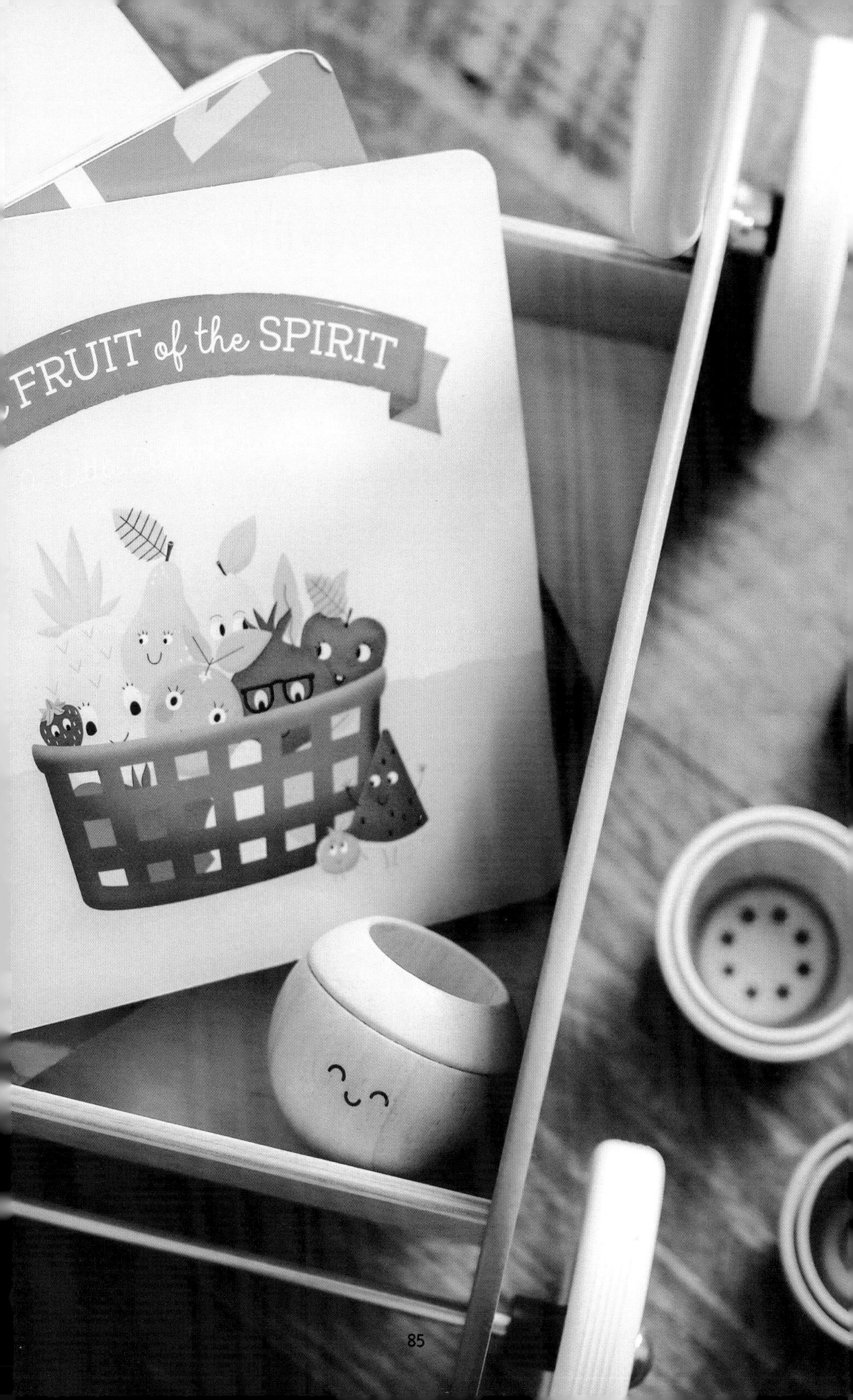
FRUIT of the SPIRIT

A Wedding

Creator of Marriage,

*What a long-awaited day today is, and
what a joy to finally say it has arrived!*

*You prepared this day before it
even came to be, Lord.*

*I praise You for Your provision and
for carefully choosing my spouse.*

*I thank You for allowing our paths to cross
and for sustaining our relationship thus far.*

*You have chosen better for me than
I could have ever dreamt up or
thought of on my own.*

Lord, You are good and do good.

*You have brought us here today to
celebrate the good gift of marriage.*

*Lord, may our marriage begin founded
and rooted in You.*

*I pray You would be the rock which
our marriage stands on.*

*I pray You would unite us in Your Spirit and
in truth and that we would depend on You
for the rest of our days.*

As we celebrate today, I pray our service would ultimately reflect the gospel at work.

I pray You would open our eyes to believe in the good news of Jesus and that many would be brought to salvation.

Give us insurmountable joy as we come together as husband and wife.

Help us to enjoy every moment of dancing and fellowship with family and friends.

Help us to cherish and serve one another in a way that reflects and honors You from this point forward.

Help us to be devoted to one another in sickness and health, in wealth and poverty, and in every circumstance we face through the years.

Grant us many years of love and faithfulness.

Use our marriage to the glory of Your name.

Amen

A New Home

Heavenly Father,

We praise You for the gift of a new home.

*We thank You for providing for us with
a roof over our heads.*

*As we begin our life in a new house, we pray
You will help us to steward it well.*

*We pray You bring lots of joy and
laughter into this home.*

*We pray for many meals and conversations
shared around the table.*

*We pray this home would welcome many
people from different backgrounds, economic
statuses, and cultures.*

*We pray that everyone who steps inside
would experience a glimpse of the gospel
through our hospitality and generosity.*

Help us to know and love our neighbors.

*Help us to serve our community and
invest in our local church.*

Lord, we pray for growth in this home.

Use every opportunity to turn our hearts to You.

*May we never get too comfortable in this home but
instead be reminded that this home is temporary.*

Keep our eyes fixed forever on eternity with You.

As we wait, Lord, bless our time in this home.

Amen

A New Friendship

Father,

What a gift we find in friendship.

*You have given us a special joy when
You give us a friend.*

*Thank You, Lord, for this new relationship
You have formed.*

I pray You use it to sharpen and refine me in the faith.

I pray You use it also for laughter and fun!

*I pray You teach us new things from the lives
of one another.*

*Help us to constantly point one another to
truth found in Your Word.*

*Help us to encourage one another and build
one another up with our words.*

*Bring us many memories that we will
treasure and hold dear.*

*Remind us of the ways You bring people together
under the banner of Your name.*

May our friendship always be founded in You.

Lord, thank You for this new friend.

Amen

Thank you for choosing this resource from The Daily Grace Co.